Five Orchestral Pieces
Op. 16

Five Orchestral Pieces
Op. 16

Arnold Schoenberg

DOVER PUBLICATIONS, INC.
Mineola, New York

Bibliographical Note

This Dover edition, first published in 1999, is an unabridged republication of *Fünf Orchesterstücke von Arnold Schönberg, Opus 16,* originally published by C. F. Peters, Leipzig, 1912. The prefatory note, glossary, and lists of contents and instrumentation are newly added.
Ernest Newman's 1914 review of *Five Orchestral Pieces* was reprinted in *Words on Music,* edited by Jack Sullivan, originally published by Ohio University Press, Athens, 1990.

International Standard Book Number: 0-486-40642-3

Manufactured in the United States of America
Dover Publications, Inc., 31 East 2nd Street, Mineola, N.Y. 11501

A REVIEW, 1914

Arnold Schönberg—one of the advanced composers of our day who make people like Richard Strauss seem quite old-fashioned—made his first appearance in London at a Queen's Hall concert on Saturday afternoon, when he conducted a performance of his *Five Orchestral Pieces.* It may be remembered that when these works were played at a Queen's Hall promenade concert in September 1912, they seemed so destitute of meaning and so full of discords that the audience laughed audibly all through the performance, and hissed vigorously at the end—which is a very unusual thing for an English audience to do, even when it is not pleased. The management was evidently apprehensive that something of the same sort might happen again on Saturday and hurt Schönberg's feelings, for in the programme there appeared the following diplomatically worded note: "Herr Arnold Schönberg has promised his co-operation at today's concert on condition that during the performance of his Orchestral Pieces perfect silence is maintained." In other words, "Don't shoot the composer; he is doing his best." It was hardly to be expected that the audience would in any case be so rude to Schönberg to his face as it had been behind his back; but as events turned out, although there was a faint hiss or titter now and then, the music was actually applauded with some warmth. The applause was evidently not merely a matter of good nature and politeness to Schönberg himself; for though he was greeted cordially when he came on the platform, smiling and looking very much alive and alert, the first of the Five Pieces was received practically in silence, the applause commencing after the second piece and increasing to the end. It was not universal, of course, and in volume was nothing like what was lavished on Tchaikovsky's Circus—and sawdust—piano concerto in B flat minor and its performer; but it was fully evident that the audience, though often puzzled, was decidedly impressed.

It was clear, indeed, that we were now really hearing the music for the first time. Perhaps it had been better rehearsed; and of course the composer knew, as no one else could know, exactly how it ought to be made to sound. Certainly I cannot imagine a greater difference between two performances of music, and the effects of them, than there was between Saturday's performance of this Schönberg work and that fifteen months ago. Only the composer, I imagine, can show them to us as they are really meant to be. They have a new orchestral feeling and technique, to which the score is only an imperfect guide. A note prefixed by Schönberg to one of the movements—to the effect that the conductor is not to concern himself with bringing out this or that voice, that seems to him important, or to soften what seems to him discords, for all this is allowed for in the orchestration, and all the conductor has to do is to see that each player employs the precise degree of force indicated in his part—I thought at first a little affected. But the music, when properly given, justifies what Schönberg says of it. The various timbres are blended in the most cunning way imaginable. Discords that on paper look unendurable and meaningless are tinted in such a way that one feels only a vague and often most alluring effect of atmosphere and distance. This is not absolutely new, of course, in orchestral music, but Schönberg's vision of the things to be done in this line, and his skill in doing them, go beyond those of any other composer I know. The third piece is quite remarkable in this respect; it does not contain a single phrase that can be called a "theme" in the ordinary significance of that term, and is a sort of shimmering, gently heaving sea of tone. It is impressionism pure and simple, and impressionism is bound to bulk more and more largely in the music of the future. It will be a little hard for us to adapt ourselves to it at first, for the very vagueness of the picture in the composer's mind, and the absence from the music of all literary or materialistically pictorial sign-posts, often destroy all the connecting links we have been accustomed to between the composer's imagination and ours. Others of these *Five Orchestral Pieces* are not impressionistic in the same way as No. 3, though what at present seems their lack of definite thematic working and clear outline is apt to make us sum them all up under the same term. There is thematic repetition in the First, but here, too, the main effect comes from the harmonic and orchestral colour and the sense of driving energy conveyed by the rhythmic motion.

But always we come back to the harmonic problem. What distinguishes all Schönberg's music since the Three Piano Pieces of Op. II from his earlier work is the apparently deliberate throwing over of the century-old distinction between consonance and dissonance. Hitherto, though we have become more tolerant each decade of discords that our predecessors would have winced under, they have justified themselves to us by standing in some sort of logical relation to a central idea of consonance. Schönberg upsets all this. He treats dissonance as a tonal language, complete and satisfying in itself, owing no allegiance, or even lip-service to consonance, either at the beginning, in the middle, or at the end of the work. It is amazing how far we can already go with him, how strangely beautiful and moving much of this music is, that, judged by the eye alone, is a mere jumble of discordant parts. But it is frankly impossible for the most advanced musician to see a coherent idea running through a great deal of this music. I do not say the coherent idea is not there, but simply that at present its coherence and its veracity are not always evident. Time alone can show whether it is our harmonic sense that thinks too slowly, or Schönberg's harmonic sense that thinks a little too rapidly for the rest of the world.

Ernest Newman
Birmingham Daily Post, 1914

CONTENTS

FIVE ORCHESTRAL PIECES
Op. 16

INSTRUMENTATION

2 Piccolos [Kleine Flöten, Kl. Fl.]
3 Flutes [Große Flöten, Fl.]
3 Oboes [Oboen, Ob.]
English Horn [Engl. H.]
4 Clarinets in D, A, B♭ ("B") [Klarinetten, Kl.]
Bass Clarinet in B♭ ("B") [Baßklarinette, Bkl.]
Contrabass Clarinet in A [Kontrabaßklarinette, Kbkl.]
3 Bassoons [Fagotte, Fag.]
Contrabassoon [Kontrafagott, Kfag.]

6 Horns in F [Hörner, Hr.]
3 Trumpets in B♭ ("B") [Trompeten, Trp.]
4 Trombones [Posaunen, Pos.]
Bass Tuba [Baßtuba, Btba.]

Percussion
    Xylophone [Xylophon, Xyl.]
    Cymbals [Becken]
    Triangle [Triangel, Trgl.]
    Tam Tam [Tamtam, Tamt.]
    Timpani [Pauke, Pk.]
    Bass Drum [Gr(osse) Trom(mel)]

Harp [Harfe, Hrfe.]
Celesta

Violins I, II [Violinen, Viol.]
Violas [Viola]
Cellos [Violoncello, Vcello]
Basses [Kontabaß, Kb.]

GLOSSARY

aber, but, though

alle = tutti

alle 3 [4, etc.] mit Dpf. [Dämpfer], all 3 (etc.) muted

allein, alone (solo)

am Steg = sul ponticello

auf beiden Fellen, on both heads [of the timpani]

auf der C [D, etc.] Saite, on the C (etc.) string

Bassstimme, bass voice [lowest line of the ensemble]

bewegte Achtel, moving 8th notes

breit(er) . . . im Ton, broad(er) . . . with a broad sound

Dämpfer, mute. "Muted" or "with mute" may appear as *mit Dämpf. . . . m. Dpf. . . . m. d(er) Dpf. . . . mit D.* or *m. D. Dämpfer auf(setzen)* = "mute on." *Dämpfer ab* = "mute off." *Dämpfer weg* = "remove mute."

das tiefe es, the low E-flat

deutlich (hervortretend), distinct, clear (to the fore)

die, the

die andere Hälfte, the other half [of the section]

die eine Hälfte, the (one) half [of the section]

die Hälfte, half [of the section]

die übrigen get(eilt), the others, *divisi*

dünn, flimsy, thin

Echotonartig, like an echo

ein, one

etwas langsamer, a little slower

eventuell Flag(eolett), possible harmonics

4 [3, etc.] fach get(eilt) = divisi a4 (etc.)

Flag(eolett), harmonic

Flatterzunge, fluttertongue

gebunden = legato

gedämpft, muted (for horn); damped (for timpani)

gest(opft), stopped (for horn)

get(eilt) = divisi

gleiche Teile, equal parts

Haupstimme bezeichnet durch ⌐ , this sign marks the principal voice [of the ensemble]

hervor(tretend), prominent, to the fore

immer, always, steadily

Klang, tone [actual sound of harmonic]

langsam(er), slow(er)

langsamer werdend, becoming slower

leicht, lightly

mässige Viertel, moderate quarter notes

mit, m., with

Mittelstimme, middle voice [of the ensemble]

Nebenstimme, secondary (accompanying) voice

nicht gebunden = non legato

nimmt, change to [a different instrument]

offen, open (for brass)

ohne, o. = senza

rasch, quick

rasch anschwellend, getting louder quickly

Saite, string

Schalltr(ichter) hoch, put the bell [of the instrument] in the air

sehr = molto

xiii

sehr gebunden = *molto legato*

sehr rasch, very quick

sehr zart (und hell), very subdued (and distinct)

so schwach wie möglich, as delicate as possible

verlangsamend bis zum Schluss, slowing down to the end

Viertel etwas langsamer, quarter notes somewhat slower

The following words accompany transitions from one note value to another:

vom Anfang, same as the beginning

von früher, the earlier

von vorher, the previous

wieder, again, once more

zart, subdued, gentle

zu2 = *a2*

zus(ammen), together

FOOTNOTES AND LONGER SCORE NOTES

I: p. 3, Fig. 4, cellos; after Fig. 5, violas:
  get. die 1. Hälfte arco [kurz, spiccato—mit Dämpfer]
      die 2. Hälfte pizz.
  divisi, 1st half *arco* (short, *spiccato*) with mute
      2nd half *pizz.*

I: p. 3, footnote (for cellos):
  Das 1. u. 2 Pult } *der Violoncelli immer der 1.*
  Das 3. u. 4 Pult } *Spieler arco, der 2. Spieler pizz.*

  Desks 1 and 2 } Cellos: At each desk, Player 1
  Desks 3 and 4 } always plays *arco,* Player 2 plays *pizz.*

I: p. 6, 1st bar, bass tuba:
  mit Dämpfer, so stark wie möglich
  muted, as strong as possible

I: p. 6, footnote (for basses):
  Das tiefe d muss dabei sein!
  The low D must be present!

II: p. 19, 3rd bar, solo viola:
  äusserst zart, die Nebenstimmen entsprechend zarter
  extremely delicate, the secondary voices correspondingly more delicate

II: p. 25, 2nd bar, English horn:
  wenn die Stelle nicht ppp möglich ist, bleibt sie weg; sie muss schwächer klingen als die Streicher
  If the passage is not possible at *ppp,* it should be omitted; it must sound softer than the strings.

II: p. 26, 2nd bar, basses:
  4 Kontrabässe stimmen die G Saite auf Gis und spielen Flag.
  4 basses tune the G string to G-sharp and play harmonics.

xiv

II: p. 28, end, violas:
alle in 2 gleichen Teilen mit Dämpfer
Tutti, divisi a2, con sordino

III: p. 29, footnote:
Es ist nicht Aufgabe des Dirigenten, einzelne ihm (thematisch)
wichtig scheinende Stimmen in diesem Stück . . . genau (subjektiv)
seinem Instrument entsprechend und nicht (objektiv) sich dem
Gesamtklang unterordnend.

*) Der Wechsel der Akkorde hat so sacht zu geschehen, dass gar
keine Betonung der einsetzenden Instrumente sich bemerkbar
macht, so dass er lediglich durch die andere Farbe auffällt.

It is not the conductor's task to call for individual voices in
this piece that seem (theoretically) important to him to be
played more prominently, or to tone down combinations that
apparently sound unbalanced. Wherever a voice is to stand
out above the rest, it is correspondingly scored and the
sounds are not to be toned down. On the other hand, it *is* the
conductor's task to take care that every performer plays at
exactly the volume prescribed; exactly (subjectively) in accor-
dance with his own instrument and not (objectively) subordi-
nating himself to the total sound.

*) The change of chords must be executed so smoothly that
absolutely no emphasis on the entering instruments can be
felt, so that the change is merely perceptible through the difference in instrumental color.

III: p. 30, Fig. 1, cellos:
4 Solo-V celli mit Dämpfer alle 4 auf der C-Saite
4 solo cellos with mute, all 4 on the C string

III: p. 32, Fig. 4, footnote:
Jede Note genau so lang aushalten, wie vorgezeichnet; aber auch
nicht länger!!!
Hold every note exactly as long as written, but not longer
either!!!

III: p. 33, 1st bar, basses:
1 fünfsaitiger Solo-Kb. auf der C-Saite
1 five-stringed solo bass on the C string

III: p. 33, 2nd bar, cellos:
III. mit auf H herabgestimmter C-Saite
No. 3 with C string tuned down to B

IV: p. 41, 1st bar, trombones:
Dieses A womöglich bringen, so stark es eben geht.
Play this A if possible, as loudly as can be done.

IV: p. 43, 1st bar, cymbals:
tremolo auf einem Beckenteller mit einem Violoncellbogen
tremolo on one cymbal with a cello bow

Five Orchestral Pieces
Op. 16

I.

*) Das 1.u.2. Pult } der Violoncelli immer der 1. Spieler arco, der 2. Spieler pizz.
**) Das 3.u.4. Pult }

*) Das tiefe d muß dabei sein!

II.

Viertel etwas langsamer.

III.

Es ist nicht Aufgabe des Dirigenten, einzelne ihm (thematisch) wichtig scheinende Stimmen in diesem Stück zum Hervortreten aufzufordern, oder scheinbar unausgeglichen klingende Mischungen abzutönen. Wo eine Stimme mehr hervorscheinen soll, als die anderen, ist sie entsprechend instrumentiert und die Klänge wollen nicht abgetönt werden. Dagegen ist es seine Aufgabe darüber zu wachen, daß jedes Instrument genau den Stärkegrad spielt, der vorgeschrieben ist; genau (subjektiv) seinem Instrument entsprechend und nicht (objektiv) sich dem Gesamtklang unterordnet.

*) Der Wechsel der Akkorde hat so sacht zu geschehen, daß gar keine Betonung der einsetzenden Instrumente sich bemerkbar macht, so daß er lediglich durch die andere Farbe auffällt.

Jede Note genau so lang aushalten, wie vorgezeichnet; aber auch nicht länger!!!

IV.

35

48
8
Gr. Fl. I. II. III.
Ob. I. II. III.
Engl. H.
I. II. Kl. in B. III.
Bkl. in B.
Fag. I. II. III.
I. III. II. V. Hr. in F. IV. VI.
Trp. in B. I. II.
I. II. Pos. III. IV. u. Btba.
I. Viol. II.
Viola.
Vcello.
Kb.
zu 3
Lallein
I.
espress.
zu 2
I. III. zu 2
alle immer mit Dämpfer
mit Dämpfer
m.D.
I. II. zu 2
alle immer mit Dämpfer III. IV. zu 2
pizz.
arco
2 Solo
alle
57
9
Gr. Fl. I.
I. Kl. in B. III.
Bkl. in B.
Fag. I.
I. II. Hr. in F. III. IV.
alle mit Dämpfer
Trp. in B. I. II. III.
alle 3 mit Dämpfer
Pos. I.
Dämpfer weg
Viol. I.
Viol. II.
Viola.
1. Solo
alle get.
stacc.

V.

Hauptstimmen bezeichnet durch ⌐.

127